EARLY LEARN TOGETH

SERIES

DISCOVERY PLA

Light and Dark

ELIZABETH LAIRD

Educational Consultant: **Carole Ritchie**

Illustrated By **Clare Beaton**

A Piccolo Original
Piccolo Books

This series has been prepared in consultation with the Pre-school Playgroups Association.

In the dark

Susie wakes up suddenly and sits up in bed.
She's just had a nightmare.
She dreamed that a giant was going to eat her.
It was horrible!
Her room is dark, and she can't see anything.
'Mum! Dad!' she calls.

Dad comes in and gives her a cuddle.
'I had bad dreams when I was little,' he says.
He turns on the light in the hall.
A bit of light comes into Susie's bedroom.
She can see that there aren't any giants now.

Have you ever had a nasty dream?

The moon and stars

Dad pulls the curtain back a bit
so Susie can see the moon.
'Why isn't the moon as bright
as the sun?' she asks.
'The sun's a ball of fire,' says Dad.
'And the moon's just made of rocks.'
'Then why does it shine at
all?' says Susie.
'The light from the sun shines
on it,' says Dad, 'and that makes
it bright and shiny.' He yawns.
'Only the side we can see is light.
The back of the moon is dark.'
'But why . . . ?' begins Susie.
'Do you mind,' says Dad,
'I want to go back to bed.
Let's talk about it in the morning.'

Creatures of the night

Susie can't sleep, so she climbs out of bed again and looks down into the street. Everything looks so different at night. The street lamps make pools of light on the ground, and the car headlights make moving shapes of light. On the other side of the street, the park is all dark.

Suddenly, Susie sees a flutter of wings.
Could it be an owl? Or a bat, perhaps?
They both like flying about at night.

Do you know the names of any creatures
that rest in the daytime and come out at night?
Do squirrels, or foxes? Or slugs and snails?

The sun

The sun has risen, and it's light again. Billy wakes up first as usual. He always wakes up earlier in the summer, because it gets light earlier. 'Ma, ba,' he says, rattling the bars on his cot.

When Susie wakes up, she remembers
the moon and stars.
She gets out of bed and runs to the window.
The park looks green now, not black,
and there are no strange shapes anywhere.

Look at the picture of the street in daytime,
then look back at the picture of it in the dark.
What can you see in the daytime that you
can't see in the night?

Bright lights and fainter lights

There's not a star to be seen now. They're still up there somewhere, and so is the moon, but the sun is so bright that all the smaller lights have disappeared.

Have you ever turned on a light in a sunny room? The electric light hardly shows at all. And have you ever shone a bright light on to the TV? Does the picture look brighter or fainter?

It's real spring weather at the moment.
A big black cloud has suddenly covered the sun, and the sky has gone darker.
What was that flash? It must be lightning!
Crash! What was that? It must be thunder!

Can you draw a picture of a thunderstorm?

Too much light

The sun's come out again.
Susie's pretending to sunbathe on a beach,
but the sun is so bright it hurts her eyes.
'I know,' says Susie. 'I need a sun-hat.'
She folds two corners of the paper together,
and sticks them down with sticky tape.

Billy wants a sun-hat too.
Susie makes one for him as quickly as she can.
He'll be after hers if she doesn't!

Could you make a sun-hat?
Can you think of anything else we use to keep off the sun when it's too strong?

Things that need light and things that don't

Mum's taken Billy and Susie out to the park.
'Why do all the daffodils point in the same direction?' says Susie.
'They all point towards the light,' says Mum.

Have you got any plants at home? Look at the leaves. Which way do they face?

Billy has turned over a big stone.
There's a worm and three slugs
sticking to it.
'They like living in dark places,'
says Mum.
'They would shrivel up in the sun.'

Why don't you turn over a stone or a brick?
You might find a creature that lives in the dark.

Shadows

It's a good day for shadows because the sun is strong.
On dull days there are hardly any shadows at all.
'Mum's shadow is the longest,' says Susie, 'then mine, and Billy's is the shortest.'

Who's got the longest shadow in your family?
And who's got the shortest?

Susie turns a corner, and skips down another path.
Her shadow runs along beside her now.
'Look,' says Susie. 'Whichever way I turn, my shadow's on the other side of me from the sun.'

Why don't you stand near a bright light and see which way your shadow falls?

Shutting your eyes

Back home again, Susie's playing a game.
She's feeling round the room
with her eyes shut.
Everything seems to be in a different place.
What's this round, warm, cuddly thing?
Oh! It's moved! It must be Billy!

Why don't you feel around with your eyes shut?

Susie doesn't want to go to bed.
She's afraid of having another bad dream.
'You won't have one tonight,' says Mum.
'How do you know?' says Susie.
'Because I've put a notice on your door,' says Mum.
'It says "No giants allowed in here." '

Try it for yourself . . .

Some things let the light through
and other things don't.
Hold a piece of paper up to the light.
Can you see it shining through?
Now hold up a book.
Does the light shine through that?

Now try a piece of thin cloth like a cotton dress.
And a piece of thick cloth, like a winter coat.
Can you see any light through them?
Be careful not to touch the light.
It's very hot and you might get burnt.

Try making a shadow clock.
You'll need to start this on a sunny morning.
Tape a piece of paper down on a sunny window sill.
Put some Plasticine round one end of a pencil
and stand it upright in the middle of the paper.
Make a mark where the shadow falls.
At lunchtime, mark the shadow again.
Do it again at supper time.
You'll see how far the shadow has moved
since breakfast.

Plants can't live without light.
They will even turn themselves towards it.

If you have any pot plants at home,
try turning them round.
Leave them for a day, then look at them again.
What have the leaves done?
Have all the plants done the same thing?

If plants have no light at all,
they lose their green colour
and go pale, or yellow.

Try putting a brick on a patch of grass.
Leave it for a day or two.
Then take it off.
What has happened to the grass under the brick?